A
Friend
Forever

Friendship defies age
and ignores distance.
It weathers the hard times
and shares the good.
Together we have found this.
Our friendship has provided
     acceptance
and understanding in a world
that pushes people apart.
But I will always remain
with the memories
of the times we have shared
knowing how fortunate I am
to be able to call you my friend.

Other books by

Blue Mountain Press INC

Come Into the Mountains, Dear Friend
by Susan Polis Schutz
I Want to Laugh, I Want to Cry
by Susan Polis Schutz
Peace Flows from the Sky
by Susan Polis Schutz
Someone Else to Love
by Susan Polis Schutz
I'm Not That Kind of Girl
by Susan Polis Schutz
Yours If You Ask
by Susan Polis Schutz
Love, Live and Share
by Susan Polis Schutz
The Language of Friendship
The Language of Love
The Language of Happiness
The Desiderata of Happiness
by Max Ehrmann
I Care About Your Happiness
by Kahlil Gibran/Mary Haskell
I Wish You Good Spaces
Gordon Lightfoot
We Are All Children Searching for Love
by Leonard Nimoy
Come Be with Me
by Leonard Nimoy
These Words Are for You
by Leonard Nimoy
Creeds to Love and Live By
On the Wings of Friendship
You've Got a Friend
Carole King
With You There and Me Here
The Dawn of Friendship
Once Only
by jonivan
Expressing Our Love
Just the Way I Am
Dolly Parton
You and Me Against the World
Paul Williams
Words of Wisdom, Words of Praise
Reach Out for Your Dreams
I Promise You My Love
Thank You for Being My Parents
A Mother's Love
gentle freedom, gentle courage
diane westlake
You Are Always My Friend
When We Are Apart
It's Nice to Know Someone Like You
by Peter McWilliams
It Isn't Always Easy
My Sister, My Friend

A
Friend
Forever

A collection of poems
Edited by Susan Polis Schutz

Blue Mountain Press ™

Boulder, Colorado

Library of Congress Number: 80-67510
ISBN: 0-88396-121-0

Manufactured in the United States of America
First Printing: October, 1980.
Second Printing: July, 1981.
Third Printing: April, 1982.

The following works have previously appeared in Blue Mountain Arts publications: "Man is forced," by Susan Polis Schutz. Copyright © Continental Publications, 1971. "Even though we live," by Susan Polis Schutz. Copyright © Continental Publications, 1978. "What created" and "We all need," by Louise Bradford Lowell. Copyright © Continental Publications, 1978. "Let us grow together" and "When we lived," by Susan Polis Schutz. Copyright © Continental Publications, 1979. "The memories that friends," by Rebecca J. Barrett. Copyright © Continental Publications, 1979. "It's uplifting to know" and "A friend like you," by Henry V. Rutherford. Copyright © Continental Publications, 1979. "It is a rare," by Ruth Langdon Morgan. Copyright © Continental Publications, 1979. "It is a special gift" and "Friendship is a special blessing," by Iverson Williams. Copyright © Continental Publications, 1979 and Copyright © Iverson Williams, 1979. "Though we are far apart," by Susan Polis Schutz. Copyright © Continental Publications, 1979, 1980. "As a friend" and "Our Friendship," by Laine Parsons. Copyright © Blue Mountain Arts, Inc., 1980. "We have something special" and "Friendship is surely," by Andrew Tawney. Copyright © Blue Mountain Arts, Inc., 1980. All rights reserved.

Thanks to the Blue Mountain Arts creative staff, with special thanks to Douglas Pagels and Jody Cone.

ACKNOWLEDGMENTS are on page 64

Blue Mountain Press INC.

P.O. Box 4549, Boulder, Colorado 80306

CONTENTS

It is a rare and special thing
to find a friend who will remain
a friend forever.

— Ruth Langdon Morgan

I want to be your friend
I want to find a link of mutual
    understanding
whether different in personality
or extreme in character;
whether self discipline allows
acceptance of actions or
tolerance of individuality.

I want to be a part of your world
and have you become a part of mine;
even though we don't see eye to eye on
all that which surrounds us —
our ideals in life
our motives for being
our reasons for existence . . .

I want to understand you;
even greater —
accept you as you are
on the basis of your life,
with an open eye
and an open heart
and as such
be a good friend.

— jonivan

a friend so rare
you stand by me no matter what
the good or bad of my life
you never disappoint me
when i need to depend on your support . . .
you tell me when i am wrong
so gently you guide me without pain
you love me even when we disagree
each day and night i feel your presence
you may not be near to touch
but you are in my mind and heart
you meet my needs so silently
i am not alone because of you
whatever i am that causes you
to love me with this loyalty . . . i pray
that i am as much for you
as you are for me
my friend i love you

— diane westlake

FRIEND

Friend, we've laughed
When humor had
Passed

Friend, you listened with
Closed lips while
Opening your heart

Friend, you felt my sorrow
And we formed one
Tear

Friend, these things
I'll remember as
The thought of you
Warms my heart.

— Lanny Allen

A Friend Like You

A friend is someone with whom
you can be completely honest
and who understands you
just the way you are.

A friend is someone to talk to
when things are going wrong
and who will give you support
in times of need.

It's wonderful to have
a friend like you.

— Henry V. Rutherford

When we lived
near each other
we participated in
the same activities
Our friendship was
strong
because we shared
so many things
Now — living apart
we rarely
see each other
but our friendship is
even stronger
because we share
the same feelings
This closeness
of hearts
is what makes
a lifetime friendship
like ours

— Susan Polis Schutz

The miracle is this . . .
The more we share
The more
We have.

— Leonard Nimoy

Friendship is a special blessing from above. It's the sharing of activities with someone who understands and cares. It's a warm ray of sunshine that fills our hearts in times of need. It's the bringing out of beautiful things in each other that no one else looked hard enough to find. It's the mutual trust and honesty that lets us be ourselves at all times.

— Iverson Williams

Our Friendship

Every day of our friendship is as exciting as the first rays of a new dawn. Time may pass and space may separate us, but distance cannot alter feelings and trust between true friends who realize that the same sun shines on us all and the same common bond is felt in the heart. As our friendship grows and days become years, we will look at our friendship as a priceless gift given to our yesterdays and waiting for our tomorrows.

— Laine Parsons

It's uplifting to know that
I can always count on you
and that you are always there
in good times and bad.
I always hoped that I would
find a person like you.
   Thank you
      for being my friend.

— Henry V. Rutherford

Man is forced to
be alone by the very
nature of society. But
if you meet a person
who is not envious,
who loves and believes
in other than himself,
then to this rare person
offer a lifetime
of friendship.

— Susan Polis Schutz

Life is sweet just because of the
friends we have made
and the things which in common
we share;
We want to live on not because
of ourselves, but because
of the people who care;
It's giving and doing for
somebody else—on that
all life's splendor depends,
And the joy of this world, when
you've summed it all up,
is found in the making of friends.

—Edgar A. Guest

We all need
a person to understand
Someone to share our
thoughts with
and always be around
in time of need
We all need
a person like you

— Louise Bradford Lowell

Though we are
farther apart
from each other
than ever
we are actually
closer
to each other
than ever
Our activities
and goals
have changed
and our homes
and daily habits
have changed
but we still
have the same
souls —
in need of
one another —
in need of
our precious
friendship

— Susan Polis Schutz

Never shall I forget
the days which I spent
with you . . .
Continue to be my friend,
as you will always
find me yours.

— Ludwig van Beethoven

You know that however much
time passes without your
hearing from me, there is not
a day that does not in some
way or other bring me nearer
to you or remind me of
your friendship.

— Felix Mendelssohn

How good it is to be blessed with a friend such as you! It is so rare . . . to find a complete person, with a soul, a heart and an imagination: so rare for characters as ardent and restless as ours to meet and to be matched together, that I hardly know how to tell you what happiness it gives me to know you.

— Hector Berlioz

The memories that friends
have made together
grow stronger
with every passing day.

— Rebecca J. Barrett

It is a special gift
from God
to find a friend
who will
remain a friend
forever.

— Iverson Williams

Our friendship has
a special meaning to me . . .
Your friendship holds a
special place in my heart.

— Anonymous

Thank you for your
presence in my life . . .
you encourage me to go
beyond myself.

— Linda Moore

Blessed are they who have the gift
of making friends,
for it is one of God's best gifts.
It involves many things but above all,
the power of going out of one's self,
and appreciating whatever is noble
and loving in another.

— Thomas Hughes

Someone like you
  makes the sun shine brighter
Someone like you
  makes a sigh half a smile
Someone like you
  makes my troubles much lighter
Someone like you
  makes life seem worthwhile.

— James W. Foley

Let us
grow together
and enrich our lives
with the friendship
we share

Let us
grow together
and enrich the world
with the love
we share

— Susan Polis Schutz

My Friend

I wish you the courage to be warm
    when the world would prefer
    that you be cool.
I wish you success sufficient to your
    needs; I wish you failure to
    temper that success.
I wish you joy in all your days; I
    wish you sadness so that you
    may better measure joy.
I wish you gladness to overbalance
    grief.
I wish you humor and a twinkle in
    the eye . . .

I wish you glory and the strength to
bear its burdens.
I wish you sunshine on your path
and storms to season your
journey.
I wish you peace — in the world in
which you live and in the
smallest corner of the heart
where truth is kept.
I wish you faith — to help define
your living and your life.
More I cannot wish you — except
perhaps love — to make all
the rest worthwhile.

— Robert A. Ward

What created the
strong hand of friendship
between us?
Our special relationship
and caring for each other
must have been
predestined by a
divine force.

— Louise Bradford Lowell

The world holds few things so wonderful as the wonder of a growth of a genuine love between two souls, deepening, broadening, intertwining all their lives, growing quite unconsciously, and in spite of full recognition of all limitations and imperfections, bringing a sense of unity of the lives, of the necessity of one to the other. Such friendships are perhaps the best proof the world affords of love at the very heart of the universe.

— Henry Churchill King

Friendship is surely one of life's special miracles. When two people are united in friendship's spirit, the relationship assumes special light and life-giving qualities unlike any other. Friendships give richness to life and promise to the future.

— Andrew Tawney

Never before
have I met a soul
so closely related to mine
or one that
so sensitively responded
to my every thought . . .
Your friendship
has become as necessary
as air.

— Peter Tchaikovsky

Friendship involves the sharing of the selves.
And one of the greatest aspects, certainly,
of love is joy in personal life.
Each friend must be able to give that joy
and to enter into it . . .
The very idea of a worthy friendship
implies that the friends need
and desire each other
and so are continuously receptive
and eager for the other's gift.

— Henry Churchill King

Keep in mind
that each of us is special
because we are different
we have come together
in this friendship
because we have our differences
to bring to each other
so listen to me
as i listen to you
we will hear ourselves
grow into the realization
of expanding mutual respect

— diane westlake

Mಚ your life
be always filled
with what you seek

May you always be friends
to the earth,
to the sky
and to the animals of both

And may I always
share with you
as openly
as you have shared with me.

— jonivan

Sharing intimately while building our lives is the most important consideration for a balanced, happy existence. Deep, meaningful friendships . . . permanent ones that grow and strengthen over many years . . . offer us security throughout the changing aspects of ourselves and the extreme acceleration of the world we live in.

— Walter Rinder

The peace of the world will in the end depend upon our capacity for friendship and willingness to use it.

— Bertha Conde

I turn to you . . .
and in your eyes
I read companionship
. . . you are
    my friend.

— Lilla Cabot Perry

There are some limited periods in my life
  where the friendships formed then
    have not lasted.
In looking back,
  I realize that these were times for me
  of isolation and turning inward,
    when I didn't share my pain
                    with anyone.
I have learned much since then.
Now I share with my friends,
  and am willing to risk
    and give of myself.
I like it better this way,
    and my friendships last . . .

— Sue Mitchell

Friends are . . .
the kisses at hellos and goodbyes,
the feeling of never having been apart
because it's so great to be together,
the knowing that you
will find each other
no matter what happens
in this world, because no barrier
is strong enough
to dare separate you.

Friends are forever.

— Edith Schaffer Lederberg

I must say, You are a friend.
Let me say no more to you,
for although I always recognized
in friendship between men
the noblest and highest relation,
it was you who embodied
this idea into its fullest reality
by letting me no longer imagine,
but feel and grasp, what a friend is.
I do not thank you, for you alone
have the power to thank yourself
by your joy in being what you are.
It is noble to have a friend,
but still nobler to be a friend.

— Richard Wagner

We have something special
that no one
    no distance
    no time
    can take away . . .
we have each other.

— Andrew Tawney

Friendship — Like music heard on the
    waters,
Like pines when the wind passeth by,
Like pearls in the depths of the ocean,
Like stars that enamel the sky,
Like June and the odor of roses,
Like dew and the freshness of morn,
Like sunshine that kisseth the clover,
Like tassels of silk on the corn,
Like mountains that arch the blue
    heavens,
Like clouds when the sun dippeth low,
Like songs of birds in the forest,
Like brooks where the sweet waters flow,
Like dreams of Arcadian pleasures,
Like colors that gratefully blend,
Like everything breathing of kindness —
Like these is the love of a friend.

— A. P. Stanley

The seeds of love
are in friendship,
and then other stages
of a relationship
develop out of that.

— Marlo Thomas

The finest kind of friendship
is between people who
expect a great deal of each other
but never ask it.

— Anonymous

Even though we live
far from each other
I always talk to you
in my thoughts
and see you
in my dreams
It doesn't matter
that we are not together
because our friendship
is such a strong part
of my life
And as long as I know that
you are happy where you are
I, too, am happy

— Susan Polis Schutz

Great lessons are learned
usually in simple and
  everyday ways . . .
What I remember is the lesson
  of friendship . . .
that it is a permanent possession.

— Pearl S. Buck

I offer you laughter
   for laughter is beauty.
I offer you honesty
   for honesty is pure.
I offer you patience
   for patience is needed to gain trust.
I offer sincerity
   for through my sincerity I will show
   you my inner being and desires . . .
All I ask in return
   is for you to be honest and open
      for through your honesty and
         openness
I will receive from you
   all that I offer.

— Roger C. Van Horn

As a friend
I've loved you lonely
and wanted you happy
I've thought of you often
and wanted to hold you
so many times
But as a dreamer
I simply hoped that you
would sense my caring
and imagined that you
would understand me
and thought that maybe
You know how much I care
though I've never taken
the time to tell you
how much you are cherished

— Laine Parsons

ACKNOWLEDGMENTS

We gratefully acknowledge the permission granted by the following authors, publishers and authors' representatives to reprint poems and excerpts from their publications.

Lanny Allen for "Friend," by Lanny Allen. Copyright © Lanny Allen, 1978. All rights reserved.

International Creative Management for "The miracle is this," by Leonard Nimoy. Copyright © Leonard Nimoy, 1979. All rights reserved.

jonivan for "I want to be your friend," by jonivan. Copyright © jonivan, 1978, 1979. And for "May your life," by jonivan. Copyright © jonivan, 1980. All rights reserved.

McCall Publishing Company for "The seeds of love," by Marlo Thomas. From "Marlo Thomas" by Mary Ann O'Roark in the August, 1978 issue of McCall's. All rights reserved.

Sue Mitchell for "There are some," by Sue Mitchell. Copyright © Sue Mitchell, 1980. All rights reserved.

Linda Moore for "Thank you," by Linda Moore. Copyright © Linda Moore, 1980. All rights reserved.

Edith Schaffer Lederberg for "Friends are . . ." by Edith Schaffer Lederberg. Copyright © Edith Schaffer Lederberg, 1980. All rights reserved.

Walter Rinder for "Sharing intimately," by Walter Rinder. Copyright © Walter Rinder, 1978. All rights reserved.

Roger C. Van Horn for "I offer you laughter," by Roger C. Van Horn. Copyright © Roger C. Van Horn, 1980. All rights reserved.

diane westlake for "a friend so rare" and "keep in mind," by diane westlake. Copyright © diane westlake, 1977. All rights reserved.

Cindy Yrun for "Friendship defies age," by Cindy Yrun. Copyright © Cindy Yrun, 1980. All rights reserved.

Contemporary Books, Inc. for "Life is sweet," by Edgar A. Guest. Reprinted from THE COLLECTED VERSE OF EDGAR A. GUEST by Edgar A. Guest, © 1934 with the permission of Contemporary Books, Inc., Chicago. All rights reserved.

Robert A. Ward for "My Friend," by Robert A. Ward. Copyright © Robert A. Ward, 1980. All rights reserved.